T0193331

Mood Swingz

by

Stephanie Nicole Tyus

Balboa Press books may be ordered through booksellers or by contacting:

Balboa Press
A Division of Hay House
1663 Liberty Drive
Bloomington, IN 47403
www.balboapress.com
844-682-1282

ISBN: 978-1-9822-6604-2 (sc)
ISBN: 978-1-9822-6603-5 (e)

Print information available on the last page.

Balboa Press rev. date: 03/22/2021

BALBOA.PRESS

Contents

Acknowledgment vii
Foreword ix
Introduction xi
My Mood Yesterday 1
Why Did You Choose Me? 2
Here We Go Again 3
My Mood Today 4
What's Next Who Have I Become 5
My Mood Tomorrow 6
Awareness 7
Smile 8
My Everyday 9
Did You Think About Me? 10

I dedicate my first project as an author to my second mother, Roberta Tyus-Pugh.

May 30, 1960
August 01, 2017

Acknowledgment

I would like to thank God, my Heavenly Father, for my life. I am truly blessed and appreciative for this opportunity to express my mood swingz as a woman of color.

Foreword

by Ronnie Eugene Doss

After reading Stephanie Nicole Tyus' book, I, Ronnie Eugene Doss, have a better perspective and viewpoint about women mood swings. I enjoyed the book.

Introduction

As sassy as I am, I must admit I enjoy my life as an everyday person I am a proud woman. Thankful for everything that I have been through in this life knowing that faith is a powerful belief. I am grateful to share my mood swingz with you to enlighten my readers with a different format and style of womanhood.

Mood Swingz is an introduction to my feelings of the past. Being a woman of color is definitely a distinction of beauty. Yet having a mental illness is a stigma of various looks, glares, thoughts, pities, and let downs.

Like every woman, I experience mood swingz that allow me to be me. My mood swingz create a new decision in my mind. That's me!

Stephanie Nicole Tyus

My Mood Yesterday

Yesterday I told you okay
I see how you handle things
yet you not going to get in my way

My mood right now is suddenly sweet
As your eyes gaze at my frame cute and petite

Knowing my style is perfection to the tee
You know your calamity aint getting to me

Yesterday it seemed so far away from today
But let you tell that everything is okay

Yesterday had hit me up for tomorrow and today
Unfortunately, I could not answer
Because I am destiny's desire

As beautiful as I am
I set all hearts fire
Oh but thank you yesterday for your cunning way
Because if it wasn't for tomorrow it would probably stay
But oh thank you yesterday
Because I woke up to realize
Today is a new day

Why Did You Choose Me?

Why did you choose me?

It's obvious to see
No, it's not beginners luck
Or would it be?

Me not knowing your objectives
Pertaining to someone like me

I guess your choice would
be from experience

Not just a lustful eye
or maybe it's my conversation
which is as pleasant as
Sweet potato pie

Why did you choose me?

Is it my hair?
Is it my feet?
Is it my frame?

I think you know what
it could be
it must be me

A gorgeous sincerity
to everyone I meet
My fate is royalty, shall
we begin

So you choose me
Not her
Nor them

Here I stand again alone
Out one a limb
Why did you choose me?

Here We Go Again

The same beat to an old tune
The sky is aquamarine
The moon an ivory tribune
Dedicated was my heart that fluttered to your every beat
A new song was bragging
I chose to retreat
Thankful enough I saw
What I needed to see
We sang a blessed song
And betrayal is how
You repaid me
Again I decided to sing
This great song
Yet and still negatively
How you chose to carry on

Girl stop
Boy no
Either which way both
Yall had to go
Yes means yes
No means no
This road has been traveled
many times before

So excuse me Sir
Pardon me Miss
But aint no way I'm
going back through this

My Mood Today

Today
Flat out
I don't play
You thought you left me
It's okay
I was gone to begin with
So you thought dedication was my path
Your outrageous outburst
is the reason to laugh
Today I am happy to be me
one hundred pounds heavier
than what I use to be
That's the only thing
morbid about me that I can see
I am beautiful in every sense
my existence is too intense
Today I chose to be
a natural work of art
even if I picked fakeness
abstract would play the part
My mood today is humble, pure and meek
Is this something you share to seek
It's a give for me
Desirable as I would be
a thick Madame
to irresistible to meet
pleasurable to the touch
today I am
Miss Never 2 Much
That's my mood today

What's Next
Who Have I Become

A New Me

A new me aint what
I used to be
because yesterday that's how I felt
A new me is what I used to be
that's how the cards were dealt
A new me is how you view me
so I claim the title
I wear the belt
A new me is what
I claim to be
Accept what it is today
A new me is how
You need to be
in a positive way

My Mood Tomorrow

Tomorrow I chase dreams
as though I were the wind
Tomorrow I finished my
race with a new
pace not knowing why
I should win

Tomorrow I change my
hair to fit new face
Tomorrow I eat according
to wise decisions not
determined by taste

Tomorrow I turn heartbreak
into a lesson no need for stressin'

Tomorrow I dance to an
new song, a new tune

Tomorrow I smile
dimples and all just
to acknowledge my thankful heart

Tomorrow I stop being tart
Tomorrow I make heartfelt
decisions with new visions
Chasing new beginnings

Tomorrow is for me
Tomorrow is for you
Tomorrow is how I felt
Yesterday and today

Awareness

Aware why stare
Aware why glare

Being me is unique
yet keeping my attention
is your defeat

Can you hang with me?
Sure!

Yet my pain you shall
not endure

Regardless to love life happiness
and such

I am aware of and
unwanted fate
We choose love
not hate

Smile

Even though the pain is
a strain on our thought
Smile

A smile is like making
our dreams run wild
Smile

Be proud to distinguish when
Be blessed to distinguish how
Smile

A smile is a perfect
place in our heart
even when voices are tart
Smile

Smile

Happiness will show
you how
Smile

My Everyday

Even when the voices
will not stop and my
mere existence is my persistence
I give no resistance
because without my
medication it can all
cease within an instance

My everyday is taken in
with kindness
yet the stigmas placed
upon me are realities
blindness I accept
the ways of this cold
world

Everyday I am thankful and blessed
including in all anguish
seclusion and stress

Sometimes it may
be a struggle to
bathe or even
get dressed

I thank my supernatural
spiritual beings
for putting me to
the test

My everyday starts
with self love
that I spread in
a contagious manner

With merit and valor
I announce myself
a success

Because without these
challenges within my
everyday

Happiness would not
be what my heart
would have to say

Did You Think About Me?

When you went shopping with my money,
did you think about me?

When you made a decision for success, a decision to be blessed,
did you think about me?

When you chose to love,
did you think about me?

When you prayed to God above,
did you think about me?

Printed in the United States
by Baker & Taylor Publisher Services